A Kid's Guide to India

The Snake Charmer of Benares (Varanasi, India)

Curious Kids Press • Palm Springs, CA
www.curiouskidspress.com

NO MATTER WHERE you go in India, you are likely to see a very cool custom among the people. They greet each other with a "namaste" (say: **nuhm**-uh-stey).

The namaste is a gesture (or movement) that involves placing both palms of your hands together in front of your chest. It is used to say hello or good-bye. It means "I bow to you; may our minds meet."

Publisher: Curious Kids Press, Palm Springs, CA 92264.
Designed by: Michael Owens
Editor: Sterling Moss
Copy Editor: Janice Ross

Copyright © 2019 by Curious Kids Press. All rights reserved. Except that any text portion of this book may be reproduced – mechanically, electronically, by hand or any other means you can think of – by any kid, anywhere, any time. For more information: info@curiouskidspress.com or 760-992-5962.

Table of Contents

Chapter 1
Welcome to India... 4
Your Passport to India.................................. 5
Where in the World Is India........................ 6
A Brief History of India................................ 8
Cool Facts About India.............................. 10
An Interview with Mahatma Gandhi......... 12

Chapter 2
People, Customs, and Traditions................ 14

Chapter 3
Landmarks and Attractions......................... 24

Chapter 4
The Animals of India................................... 30

Glossary 45
For Parents and Teachers............................ 49

Photo: Taj Mahal by Amal Mongia

Chapter 1

Welcome to
INDIA

The unique Border Security Force Camel Contingent during the annual Republic Day Parade.

HOW MUCH DO YOU KNOW about the country of India? Take this quiz to find out.

True or False

1. In most parts of the country, it is against the law to kill a cow.

2. India is the only country in the world that has both lions and tigers in the wild.

3. Until 1950, all Hindu people in India were divided into social ranks, called *castes*.

If you said "true" to all three questions, you are well on your way to knowing a little bit about this fascinating country. But there is much more to know. Turn the page to start learning more about this amazing country.

Your Passport to India

Official Name: Republic of India
Capital City: New Delhi
Country Area (Size): 1,269,219 sq. mi. (3,287,263 sq. km); seventh largest in the world.
Population: 1,354,051,854 (second largest in the world).
Official Languages: Hindi, English, plus 21 others
Money: Indian rupee
Independence Day: August 15

Did You Know?
China is the only country in the world that has more people than India.

THE NATIONAL FLAG OF INDIA has three horizontal stripes. The orange stripe stands for courage. The white stripe represents truth. The green stripe represents life and **prosperity**.

In the middle of the white stripe is a navy blue **symbol** of a wheel with 24 spokes. The spokes represent 24 qualities of a person, such as service, forgiveness, and love.

5

Where in the World is India?

Map labels: AMRITSA, PAKISTAN, Rajasthan, NEW DELHI, Taj Mahal, CHINA, NEPAL, Sikkim, BHUTAN, VARANASI, Sanchi, BANGLADESH, KOLKATA, MYANMAR, Sun Temple, Ajanta & Ellora Caves, MUMBAI, Bay of Bengal, Arabian Sea, GOA, CHENNAI, KOCHI, SRI LANKA, Indian Ocean

INDIA IS LOCATED in southeast Asia. It is bordered by the Great Himalayan mountains in the north, the Indian ocean in the south, the Bay of Bengal to the east, and the Arabian Sea to the west. It also borders seven other countries: Pakistan, China, Nepal, Bhutan, Myanmar, Bangladesh and Sri Lanka

Flying to India

EVERY YEAR, nearly nine million tourists visit India from all over the world. Imagine. That's like every person in the state of New Jersey going to India in one year. Here's how long it takes to fly to India from New York City, London, or Sydney, Australia.

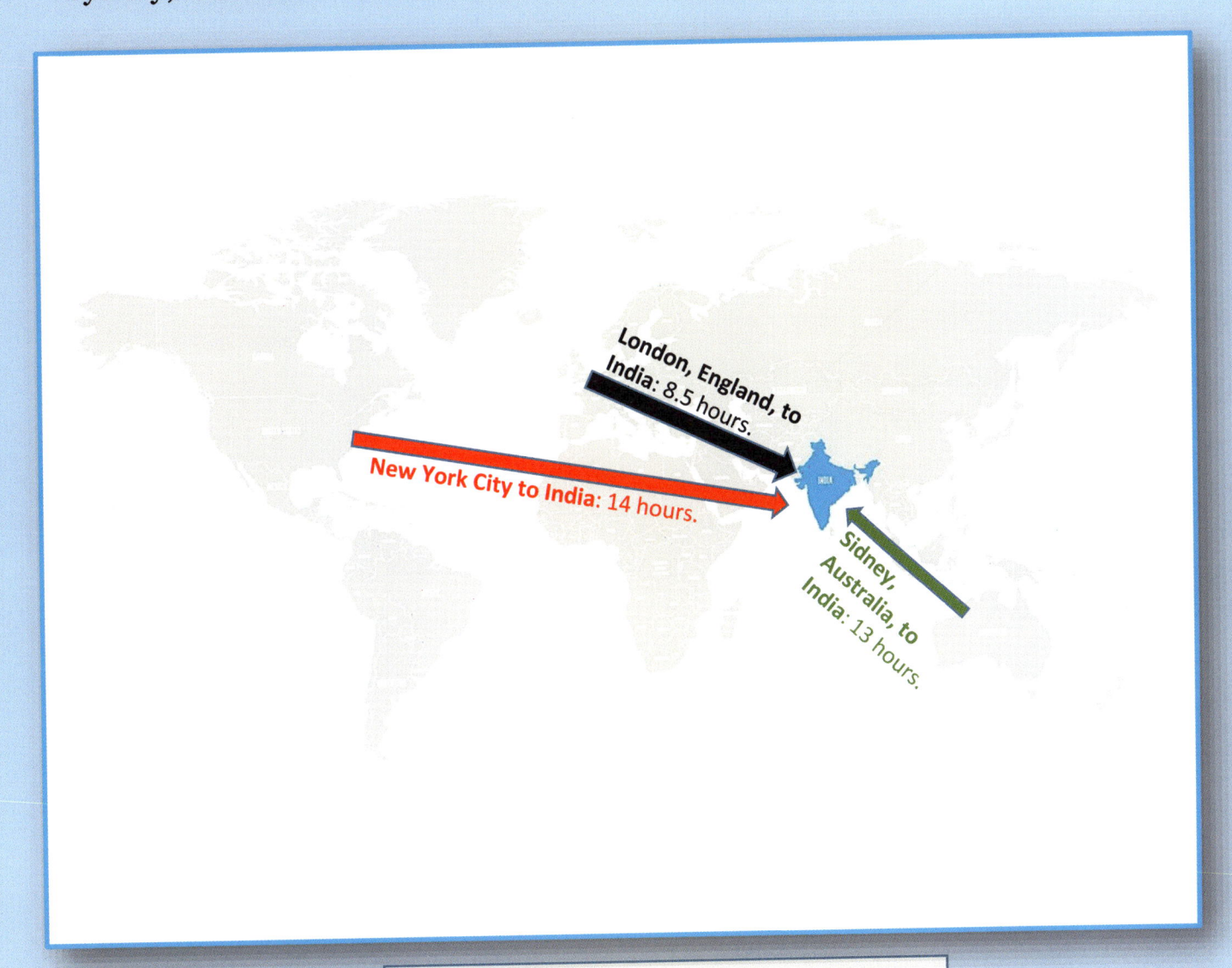

London, England, to India: 8.5 hours.

New York City to India: 14 hours.

Sidney, Australia, to India: 13 hours.

Did You Know?

Calcutta was the capital of British India from 1833 to 1912. Today, it is the second largest city in India. It is known as "the City of Palaces."

A Brief History of India

INDIA HAS A VERY LONG HISTORY. The first settlements were built in the area now known as India more than 9,000 years ago.

More recently, India's history can be divided into three distinct periods:

1757 to 1858: The Rule of the East India Company

1858 to 1947: The Rule of the British Crown (aka the British Raj)

1947 to present: Free and Modern Period

Here is a brief look at major events of these three periods.

The Rule of the East India Company (1757 to 1858)

1600: Queen Elizabeth I grants the East India Company a charter (or permission) to conduct trade in the Indian Ocean region.

1740-1800: The East India Company gradually seizes control over large parts of the Indian subcontinent (a southern region and peninsula of Asia).

1857: The Indian Rebellion (also known as India's First War of Independence) begins. As a result, the British government takes control under the rule of British Raj. (The word "Raj" in the Hindi language means government.)

The Rule of the British Crown (1858 to 1947)

1858: Queen Victoria of England takes over the rule of India, establishing the British Raj (kingdom).

1869: Mahatma Gandhi, India's Father of the Nation, is born.

1876: Queen Victoria is crowned Empress of India, the largest colony under British rule.

8

The Rule of the British Crown (1858 to 1947)

1920: Mahatma Gandhi begins nonviolent protests for independence.

1848-1947: Great Britain rules all of India.

1947: India establishes its independence from Great Britain.

The Free and Modern Period (1858 to 1947)

1947: India becomes an independent nation. Jawaharlal Nehru is elected the first Prime Minister of India

1948: Mahatma Gandhi is assassinated.

1950: The Constitution of India, which is the supreme law of India, becomes effective; India becomes a republic.

1964: Nehru dies.

1966: Nehru's daughter, Indira Gandhi, is elected primer minister.

1984: Indira Gandhi is assassinated. Her son Rajiv Gandhi takes over.

1991: Rajiv Gandhi is assassinated.

2007-2012: Pratibha Patil becomes the first female president of India.

2014: Narendra Modi is sworn in as prime minister to India.

Did You Know?
India has both a president and a prime minister. The president is known as the first citizen of India. However, he or she has little power. It is merely a **figurehead** position. The real power is held by the Primer Minister.

Cool Facts About India

THE HIMALAYAS form a mountain range across five countries: Nepal, India, Bhutan, China, and Pakistan (see map). The Himalayan range has many of Earth's highest peaks, including Mount Everest.

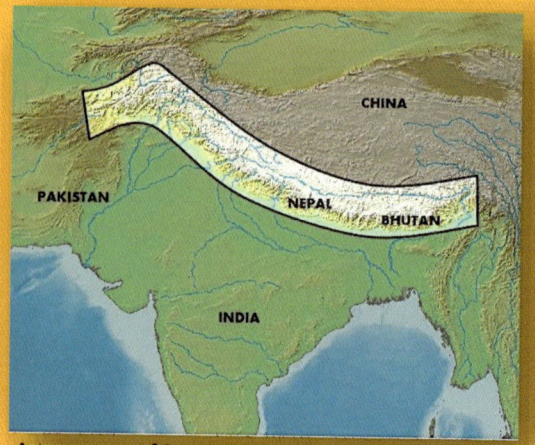

Art courtesy of Sven Manguard

Quick Quiz
What is money in India called?
(a) Ruble
(b) Rupee
(c) Peso

(Answer: Page 5)

Did You Know?
The idea of shampooing your hair was invented in India. But they didn't use the liquid kind of shampoo that you use today. They used herbs. The word 'shampoo' comes from an old Indian language word *champu,* which means "to massage."

The popular kids' board game called *Chutes and Ladders* in the United States is based on an ancient Indian board game called *Snakes and Ladders*.

Today, India is both a very rich country as well as a very poor country. (About one-third of the people in India live on less than $1.25 a day.)

Religion
More than 80 percent of the people in India are Hindu. Hindu is a major world religion that was started in India. It is different from other major religions in one particular way. There is no single founder of Hinduism. The religion is based on ancient writings, which are considered **sacred**.

Indian actress Priyanka Chopra, wife of musician Nick Jonas, wears a green bindi in the picture.

Photo: Bollywood Hungama

BINDI

Married women in India often wear a colored dot, called a "bindi," in the middle of their forehead. Why?

A Hindu tradition says that all people have a third inner eye. The two physical eyes are used for seeing the outside world (or the actual world around them). The third inner eye focuses inward toward God.

The colored dot serves as a constant reminder to keep God at the center of one's thoughts.

Bollywood

In the United States, Hollywood is known as the capital of the film industry. Every year, around 700 movies are made in Hollywood.

But Hollywood is not the biggest film industry in the world. That title goes to BOLLYWOOD.

Bollywood is the name of the film industry in India. But it's not a real place. It is based in the city of Mumbai (formerly called Bombay).

Bollywood got its name by combining Bombay and Hollywood.

Dig In!

In India, it is considered perfectly okay to eat with your hands. In fact, in a lot restaurants, you won't even get a fork or knife. But just remember: when eating with your fingers, make sure you use only your right hand. The left hand is considered to be "unclean."

The Hindi language is made up of 33 consonants and 11 vowels. You read from left to right.

What's to Eat?

Many Hindus are vegetarian. They don't eat beef or other meat. But some Hindus will eat lamb and chicken.

11

An Interview With Mahatma Gandhi

MAHATMA GANDHI WAS ONE of the great civil rights leaders of India. In many ways, he was like Martin Luther King, Jr. in the United States or Nelson Mandela in South Africa. He also led the fight for Indian independence from the British Empire. Here is an imaginary (or make-believe) conversation with this great leader. What would you want to ask Mahatma Gandhi if you could?

Is Mahatma your real first name?

No. My real first name was Mohandas. But in 1914 in South Arica, I was given the title mahatma, which means great soul.

Did you have any children?

Yes, my wife and I had four boys.

How did you become a civil rights leader?

When I was 23 years old, I went to South Africa. I saw a lot of **discrimination** there. Laws for people with dark skin were different than laws for people with light skin. I wanted to help change those unfair laws.

I read that you were a vegetarian. Is that true?

Yes, but once for five years, I ate nothing but fruits, nuts and seeds. I switched back to vegetarianism after I had some health problems.

How old were you when you got married?

I was 13. That may seem strange today, but in India back then, it was quite common.

What did you want to teach people?

I never thought I had anything new to teach the world. Truth and nonviolence are two principles I lived by. And those principles are as old as the hills.

Chapter 2

People, Customs, And Traditions
Cows

EVERYWHERE YOU GO in India, you are sure to see cows – lots of them. They wander freely in both rural areas and city streets. Why? Eighty percent of the people of India are Hindus. For many Hindus, the cow is a **sacred** or holy animal. It cannot be hurt. It can't be killed or eaten. It symbolizes (or represents) strength. It also gives life-giving milk. Don't be surprised if you see people bowing to a cow in India.

Castes

FOR THOUSANDS OF YEARS, the people of India were divided into four different groups, known as **castes**. Castes kept people separated. Caste members lived, ate, married, and worked with others in their own group. Kids in one caste could not play with kids from another caste. Young people in one caste could not marry someone from another caste.

There was also a fifth group of people. They were outside of castes. They were known as untouchables or outcastes. They had no rights. Often, the only way they could get money was by begging. If they did have a job, it was always a dirty job, something no one else wanted to do, such as getting rid of dead animals.

India's civil rights leader, Mahatma Gandhi, called these people Harijan ("Children of God"). But many of the Harijan today prefer to be called Dalit, a word that means "**oppressed**."

Today, the caste system is against the law. In cities, people of all castes meet socially or for business. But many people still **discriminate** based on the caste system.

Poor family in slum area of Delhi.

People, Customs, and Traditions, cont.

Snake Charmer

FOR HUNDREDS OF YEARS, snake charmers could be found at festivals and bazaars throughout India. They would play a flute and "charm" the snake into dancing along with the music.

But here's a little-known secret. Snakes don't have ears. They can't hear. So what the snake is doing is simply swaying to the movement of the flute.

Hindus have a great deal of respect for snakes. But in 1972, India passed a law that **forbid** anyone to keep a snake. Nevertheless, the law hasn't been enforced.

Diwali: The Festival of Lights

DIWALI is India's biggest and most important holiday of the year. It is known as the festival of lights. For Hindus, Diwali is as important as Christmas is to Christians.

The word Diwali means "row of lights." At the beginning of the five-day festival, Hindus put clay lamps outside their homes. The lamps symbolize the triumph of good over evil.

The date of Diwali changes each year. But usually it falls between October and November. During the festival, people exchange gifts; they get together for prayer; and they enjoy huge feasts, often followed by amazing fireworks.

The festival also marks the beginning of the Hindu New Year. In a way, Diwali is sort of like the 4th of July, Thanksgiving, Christmas, and New Year's all rolled into one.

Lighting candle and clay lamps during Diwali night.

People, Customs, and Traditions, cont.

Clothing

Many women in India wear a colorful silk garment called a *sari*. The word *sari* in Sanskrit (an old Indian language) means "strip of cloth." It is worn with a *choli*. That's sort of like a t-shirt. It is a garment that covers from the neck to the waist.

A sari is a single piece of cloth. Typically, the sari is wrapped around the waist with the loose end of the cloth worn over the shoulder.

Men often wear a garment called a *dhoti*. That is a piece of cloth that is tied around the waist and legs. Men also wear a *kurta*, a loose shirt that is worn about knee-length.

Shubha Khote is an Indian film and television actress wearing a sari

Man wearing a kurta and dhoti

18

Sports in India: Kabaddi

DO YOU LIKE TO PLAY "Capture the Flag" with your friends? If so, then you'll probably also like one of India's favorite sports. It's called kabaddi. The word kabaddi comes from an Indian language word meaning "to hold hands."

The game is played with two teams on opposite sides of a field. Individual players take turns crossing onto the other team's side. That player, called a "raider," tries to "tag out" as many of the players as he or she can before returning home without being tackled. Oh, they also must do it all in a single breath, while yelling "kabaddi, kabaddi"!

Points are scored for each player tagged. The opposing team earns a point for stopping the raider.

Kabaddi is one of the most popular games in India. It got its start in India in the early 1900s.

The first Kabaddi World Cup was in Mumbai (Bombay) in 2004. Teams from Asia Europe and North America competed. Guess who won?

Fun Fact
Parcheesi is considered India's "national game." But kids also like to play other board games, like Backgammon. Outside, they play soccer or badminton. They also love to fly kites.

Playing Kabaddi at a beach in India

People, Customs and Traditions, cont.

YOGA

HAVE YOU EVER TRIED to turn your body into a slithering snake, or balance on one leg like a flamingo, or stand like a warrior? If so, you already know a little bit about yoga.

In a way, yoga is like a set of exercises. The exercises involve both your body and your mind. They help make you relax and feel peaceful.

Yoga exercises involve poses. There are many different poses in yoga. For example, standing stiff like a tall oak tree is a pose. Lying flat on the floor and raising your upper body like a cobra is another pose.

Kids throughout the world practice yoga. But did you know that yoga got its start in India thousands of years ago? It was developed as a way to achieve peace between the heart and soul.

Here are some popular yoga poses. Can you match each numbered pose to the name of the pose below?

High lunge ____	Meditation ____
Downward facing dog ____	Cobra pose ____
Tree pose ____	Plow ____

Answers: High lunge: 6, Downward facing dog: 2, Tree pose: 4, Meditation: 5, Cobra pose: 1, Plow: 3

People, Customs and Traditions, cont.

Maharaja

IN 1947, INDIA GAINED its independence from Great Britain. At the time, there were more than 600 "princely states" in India. A princely state was ruled by a native Indian prince or ruler, called a *maharaja*. But the British still had control over the prince.

Maharaja comes from two Sanskrit words. (Sanskrit is an ancient Indian language.) "Maha" means "great." "Raja" means "King." The female equivalent to Maharaja is Maharani. It was a title used either by the wife of a maharaja or by a woman ruling in her own right.

The maharajas were extraordinarily wealthy. They owned palaces, jewels, Rolls Royce automobiles, and much more.

After independence, the maharajas were allowed to keep their property. They also received a "privy purse" or allowance from the government.

But that all changed in 1971. The government of India **abolished** the title maharaja. It took away the maharaja's allowance. It also forced them to pay taxes, something they never had to do before.

Suddenly, many maharajas were forced to sell their assets (the things they owned). Some ended up very poor.

But other former maharajas were good businessmen They turned their palaces into hotels. They started museums with their collections of arts. Today, they are still very wealthy.

Maharaja in Patiala, India

23

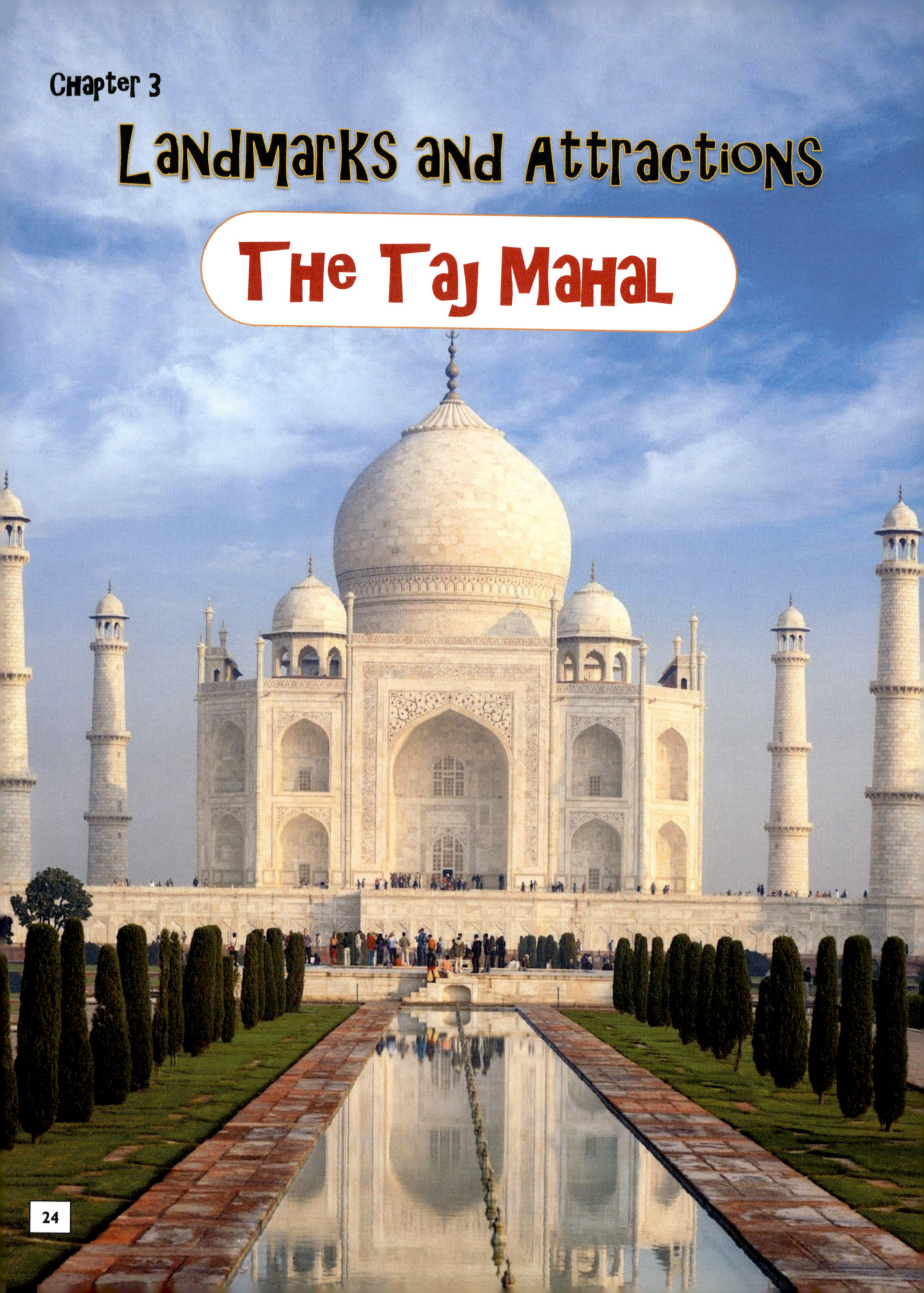

Chapter 3
Landmarks and Attractions
The Taj Mahal

THE TAJ MAHAL is a huge palace and mausoleum in Agra, India. But it is also a symbol of a great love story.

The story begins in 1607. That year, a young prince in India, named Shah Jahan, saw a young princess. It was love at first sight. He was 14 years old and she was 15.

Five years later, in 1612, the two were married, and in 1628, Shah Jahan became the emperor of India. He then gave the woman he loved the name Mumtaz Mahal, meaning "Jewel of the Palace."

Although Shah Jahan had other wives, Mumtaz Mahal was his favorite. She went with him everywhere. But then in 1631, tragedy struck. Mumtaz Mahal gave birth to the couple's 14th child. Soon after, she died. Shah Jahan was overcome with grief.

He decided to build the world's most beautiful monument in memory of the woman he loved. More than 22,000 workers and 11,000 elephants worked night and day to construct the mausoleum. But it still took 22 years to build.

When Shah Jahan died in 1666, his body was placed in a tomb next to the tomb of Mumtaz Mahal. This magnificent monument came to be known as "Taj Mahal."

THE TAJ MAHAL
At-a-Glance
What: Palace
Where: Agra, India
Height: 240 feet (73 m)
Completed: 1653
Annual Visitors: 7 to 8 million.

Shah Jahan

Mumtaz Mahal

Landmarks and Attractions, cont.

Ranthambore National Park

WOULD YOU LIKE TO SEE the magnificent Bengal tiger in its natural habitat?

There is a special place in India where you can do that. It's called Ranthambore National Park.

Many years ago, the park was the favorite hunting grounds for India's Maharaja of Jaipur. A maharaja (say: mah-huh-rah-juh) was a Hindu prince or ruler. Jaipur is the capital of Rajasthan, one of India's 29 states.

But in 1980, the India government made the grounds a national park. Today, it is 151 sq. miles (392 sq. km) or a little more than twice the size of Washington, D.C. (It's also about the same as 73,000 football fields, if you can imagine that.)

Tigers aren't the only animals you can see in the park. You will also find everything from leopards and hyenas to Indian mole rats and porcupines. There are also crocodile-filled lakes.

The Pink City

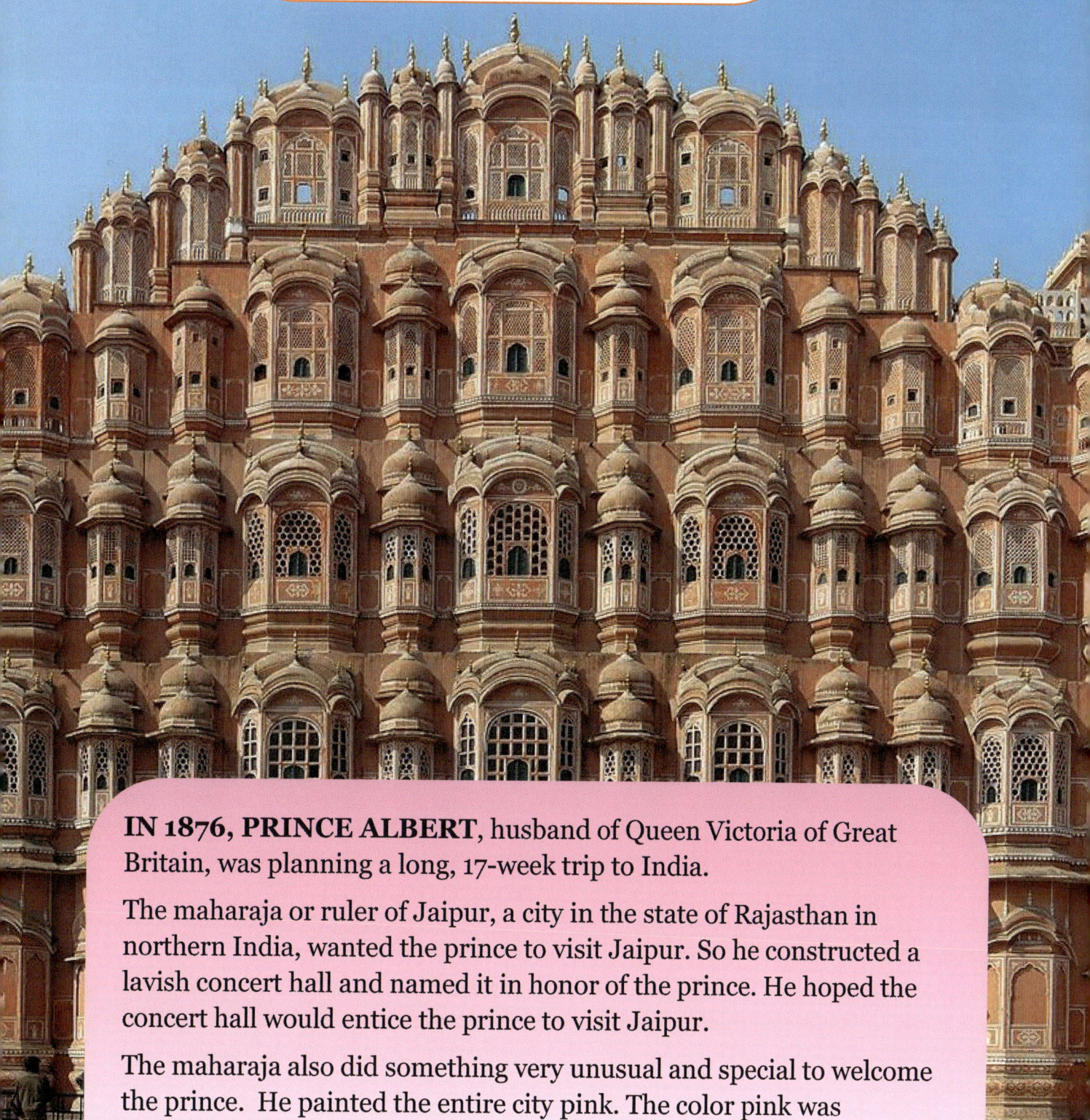

IN 1876, PRINCE ALBERT, husband of Queen Victoria of Great Britain, was planning a long, 17-week trip to India.

The maharaja or ruler of Jaipur, a city in the state of Rajasthan in northern India, wanted the prince to visit Jaipur. So he constructed a lavish concert hall and named it in honor of the prince. He hoped the concert hall would entice the prince to visit Jaipur.

The maharaja also did something very unusual and special to welcome the prince. He painted the entire city pink. The color pink was considered the color of **hospitality.**

Today, there is a law in Jaipur that says all buildings and homes must be painted pink. Many people refer to Jaipur as simply "the Pink City."

Landmarks and Attractions, cont.

The Ganges River

THE GANGES (gan-jees) RIVER is one of the two most important rivers in India. It is 1,560 miles (2,510 km) long, starting in the Himalayan mountains.

In the Hindu religion, the water of the Ganges is considered sacred. Hindu people from all over travel to the Ganges to bathe in the water. They believe the water will cleanse them (or rid them) of any bad deeds or sins.

In the summer months, many tourists find the Ganges a fun river to go rafting.

Sadly, this important and magnificent river has a great deal of **pollution**. More than 400 million people live close to the river. They use it to wash and bathe and cook in. Many cities along the river dump their **sewage** into the river. As a result, many illnesses in India are caused by water-borne diseases.

The Camel Festival

CAN YOU IMAGINE a beauty contest for camels?

That's just one of the crazy-fun events at the largest camel fair in the world.

It's held every year in India from late October to early November. Thousands of people from all over the world attend the fair.

In many ways, a camel festival is like a country fair in the United States. People sell their livestock, including camels, horses, sheep and goats. Other people sell their handicraft, including bracelets and colorful clothes, at the crafts **bazaar**.

There are also camel-cart rides, folk dancing, horse dancing competitions, and "best moustache" contest. There are even hot-air balloon rides. And, of course, like any fair, there is food . . . lots of it.

There is also one other thing at camel fairs that you probably won't see at a country fair in the U.S. -- **snake charmers**.

The fair takes place on the banks of the Pushkar Lake. Toward the end of the festival, people bathe in the waters of the lake. Many people believe that this special ceremony helps wash away their sins.

At the end of the fair, there is a huge fireworks display. Now that's something you just might see at a country fair.

Chapter 4

The Animals of India

Snow Leopard

IF YOU EVER GO TO INDIA, hoping to see the snow leopard, don't hold your breath. This beautiful animal is rarely seen – at least in the wild. In fact, snow leopards are often called "the ghosts of the mountains."

Snow leopards live in the mountain regions of central and southern Asia. In India, they live in parts of the western Himalayas.

Few people would want to live where snow leopards live. Their ideal **habitat** is cold and **desolate**.

Since it is so **elusive,** no one knows exactly how many snow leopards are left in the world. Scientists estimate that there are probably fewer than 500.

The Roar of the Lion

Big cats like lions, tigers, and jaguars, and leopards all ROAR – all, that is, except for the snow leopard. It cannot roar. It can only hiss, growl, and wail.

THE SNOW LEOPARD
At a Glance

Length: 30 to 59 in. (75 – 130 cm)
Height at the Shoulder: About 22 in. (56 cm)
Tail Length: 31 to 41 in. (80 to 105 cm)
Weight: 49 to 121 lb. (22 to 55 kg)
Diet: Carnivore (meat eater)
Lifespan: 15 to 20 years

The Animals of India, cont.

The Indian Elephant

THE INDIAN ELEPHANT is one of three kinds of Asian elephants. Asian elephants are different from African elephants (see box below).

Asian elephants usually live in groups of six or seven females, led by the oldest female, the **matriarch.**

They spend most of their day eating grasses, tree bark, roots, and small stems. But they really love bananas, rice, and sugarcane.

Even though Asian (or Indian) elephants are slightly smaller than African elephants, they are still the largest living mammals on earth.

ASIAN ELEPHANT At-a-Glance

Height: 6 ½ to 11 ½ ft (2 to 3.5 m)
Weight: Around 11,000 pounds (about 5,000 kg)
Lifespan: 60 to 70 years
Diet: Grasses, weeds, and leafy plants.

5 Ways Asian Elephants Are Different from African Elephants

- They are smaller.
- They have one "finger" at the tip of their trunk. (African elephants have two "fingers.")
- They're generally shorter than African elephants.
- They have smaller ears.
- They weigh less than African elephants.

33

The Animals of India, cont.

Indian Camel

QUICK QUIZ: What has large eyes with long eyelashes, bushy eyebrows, small ears, and two toes on each foot?

If you said "an Indian camel," you're right.

Indian camels, also known as Dromedary camels, are a little different from other camels. The main difference is that they have a single hump, rather than two humps like other camels. They also have a heavy growth of hair on their throat.

Most of India's camels live in the state of Rajasthan, one of the most beautiful states in the country. They are used as a means of transportation for both people and goods. They also provide humans with milk.

THE INDIAN CAMEL
At a Glance

Height: Up to 6 ½ feet (2 m) tall at the shoulder.
Weight: Up to 1,320 pounds (600 kg)
Diet: Herbivorous, including thorny plants and dry grasses.
Lifespan: 40 to 50 years

Did You Know?
Camels can go without food for three or four days.

The Animals of India, cont

One-Horned Rhino

THE GREATER ONE-HORNED RHINO (aka the "Indian rhino) is the largest of all rhinos. Yet, by the beginning of the 21st century, it was almost **extinct**. There were fewer than 200 in India.

Fortunately, India passed a law that made it **illegal** to hunt rhinos. Today, there is as estimated 3,600 of these magnificent animals in the wild.

ONE-HORNED RHINOCEROS
At a Glance

Length: 10 – 12.5 feet (3.0 – 3.8 m), head and body.
Height at shoulder: 5.75 – 6.5 feet (1.75 – 2.0 m)
Weight: 4,000 – 6,000 lbs. (1,800 – 2,700 kg)
Diet: Mostly grasses, but also leaves, branches of shrubs and trees.
Lifespan:
Status: Vulnerable (fewer than 3,600 in the wild), mainly as the result of **poaching**.

Did You Know?
The horn of a rhinoceros is made of *keratin*. Your fingernails are also made of keratin. In most adult rhinos, the horn reaches a length of between 8 to 24 inches (20 to 61 cm).

Fun Fact
The word rhinoceros comes from two Greek words: rhino, meaning nose, and ceros, meaning horn.

The Animals of India, cont.

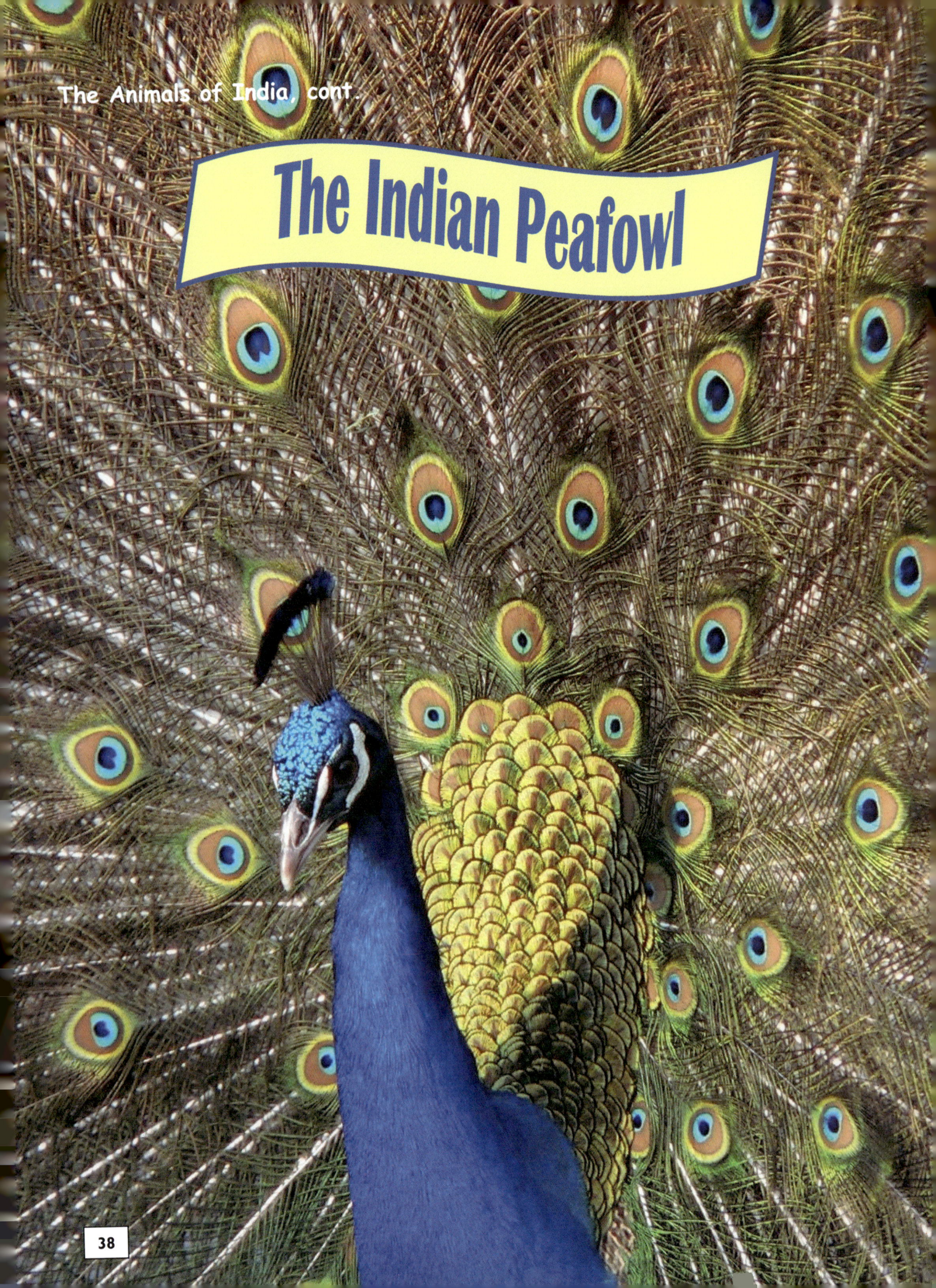

The Indian Peafowl

IF YOU'RE LIKE MOST PEOPLE, you probably call them peacocks. But that name is just for males. The female is called a peahen. Both are known as peafowl.

The peacock (the male) is one of the most beautiful birds on Earth. Its tail feathers spread out into a magnificent fan, which features many colorful "eyes" of blue, green, gold, and other colors.

The peahen, on the other hand, is really kind of dull. It is basically a drab brown color. But there is a reason for that. The peahen is less colorful because she needs to blend in with the environment when she is **incubating** her eggs.

In India, the peafowl is protected. It is a sacred bird. That's because Hindus believe the spots on the peacock's tail symbolize (or represent) the eyes of the gods.

BTW, baby peacocks (or peahens) are called peachicks. And a group of peafowl is called a "party" or a "pride."

The Indian Peacock At-a-Glance

Average Weight (male): 8 – 13 lbs. (4-6 kg); (female): 6 to 8 lbs. (3 – 4 kg)
Length (bill to tail): (male): 39–45 inches (100-115 cm); (female): up to 37 inches (95 cm)
Wingspan: (1.8 m)
Tail Length: Up to 19.9 inches (50.5 cm)
Lifespan: 15 years (in the wild)
Diet: Omnivorous. (They eat seeds, insects, fruits, and small reptiles.)

The Animals of India, cont.

Gray Langur

THE GRAY LANGUR monkey has the perfect name. That's because the word "langur" means "having a long tail." The gray langur's tail is more than 3 feet (about 1 m) long.

Langurs spend half their time on the ground and the other half in trees. (But they can also be found in many villages and towns in India.) They sleep at night and spend the day looking for food or **grooming** themselves.

They make a number of different sounds, including harsh barks when a **predator** is around, honks when groups are fooling around together, and even hiccups when they first find another group. They walk around in a "quadrupedal" manner. That means they use all four limbs to move about.

Since they are considered sacred by Hindus, they are left alone – even when they are raiding shops for food.

Gray langurs have silver fur and black faces, fingers, toes, and ears.

Gray Langur At-a-Glance

Head and Body Length: Up to 31 inches (70 cm).

Tails: Up to 40 inches (102 cm).

Males are larger than females.

Weight: About 40 lbs. (18 kg).

Diet: Primarily herbivores (but will also eat bamboo, mosses, and fruits).

Lifespan: About 20 years.

Other: India has a law against capturing or killing Gray Langurs.

Did You Know?
Langurs can leap up to 15 feet (4.7 m) straight up).

Royal Bengal Tiger

ROYAL BENGAL TIGER
At a Glance
The National Animal of India

Length: (male) Up to 9.8 feet (3 m); (female): up to 8.5 feet (2.6 m)

Average Weight: (male) Up to 485 pounds (220 kg); (female) up to 308 pounds (140 kg)

Diet: Carnivorous

Average Speed: 35-40 mph (49-65 km/h)

Lifespan: 15 years in their national habitat.

Predators: Humans. People have hunted tigers for years and destroyed their habitats.

Conservation Status: Endangered. (India has only about 2,000 Bengal tigers in the wild.)

Male tiger and mugger crocodile at Ranthambore National Park.

Did You Know?
No tiger has the same pattern of stripes on its body as any other tiger.

The Animals of India, cont.

The Tigress Queen of India

She was the most photographed tigress in the world. For more than 20 years, people came to India from around the world just to get a picture of her. She was known as the Tigress Queen of India.

Her real name was Machli, which means fish. That may seem like a strange name for a tiger. But she got the name because she had a fish-shaped mark on the left ear of her face.

Her popularity helped raise millions of dollars for the Indian government. As a way to thank her (and honor her), the Indian government gave her a "Lifetime Achievement Award." It also issued a stamp with her picture.

Sadly, she died at the age of 20 in 2016. She was the world's oldest-surviving tigress in the wild. (The average lifespan of most tigers in the wild is 10 to 15 years.) Today, her children and grandchildren still roam the park.

Glossary

abolish (*verb*): To end or stop; to do away with.

assassinate (*verb*): The act of murdering someone by a surprise attack.

bazaar (*noun*): A street market, often found in the Middle East.

desolate (*adjective*): Bleak, barren. Without things usually necessary for life.

domesticated (*noun*): Tamed; opposite of wild.

discriminate (*verb*): To treat certain people or groups differently from other people or groups.

elusive (*adjective*): When referring to animals: Hard to find or catch.

extinct (*adjective*): No longer in existence; no longer living.

figurehead (*noun*): The head of an organization or government with no real power.

forbid (*verb*): To prevent or prohibit.

grooming (*verb*): Cleaning, washing, brushing.

habitat (*noun*): The place or environment where a plant or animal normally lives and grows.

hospitality (*noun*): A friendly and generous treatment of guests.

illegal (*noun*): Not allowed or permitted; unlawful.

incubating (*noun*): Keeping (eggs) warm until time to hatch.

independence (*noun*): Freedom from outside control; the ability to make one's own decisions.

mammal (*noun*): A type of animal that feed its babies from its mother's milk.

matriarch (*noun*): A woman who acts as the head of a family or tribe.

pollution (*noun*): The action of making something unsafe or unsuitable for use.

predator (*noun*): An animal that lives by killing or eating other animals.

prosperity (*noun*): The condition of being successful, usually by making money.

sacred (*adjective*): Blessed, holy; worthy of worship.

symbol (*noun*): Something that represents or stands for something else.

Namaste! Hope you enjoyed visiting INDIA!

Explore the World

Find these books on Amazon.com
Preview them at curiouskidspress.com

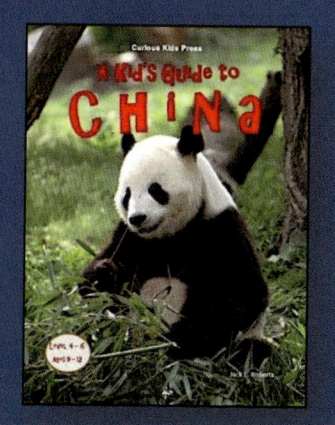

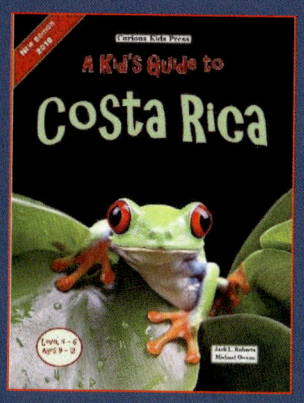

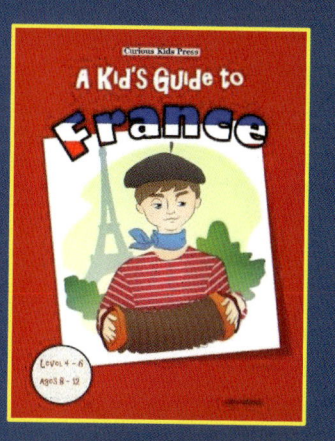

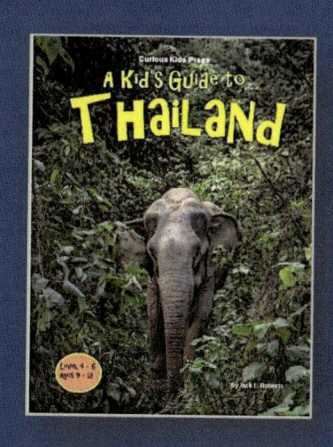

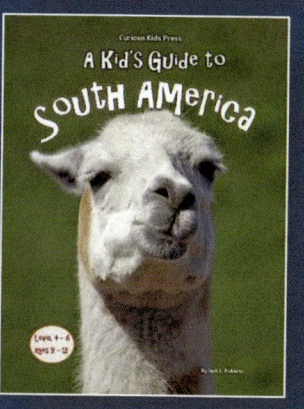

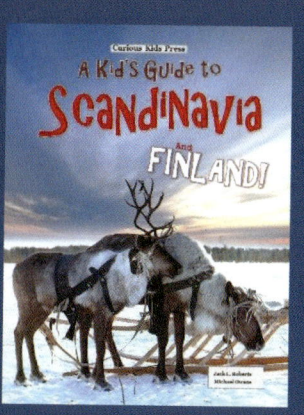

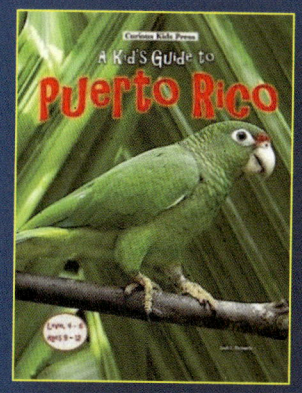

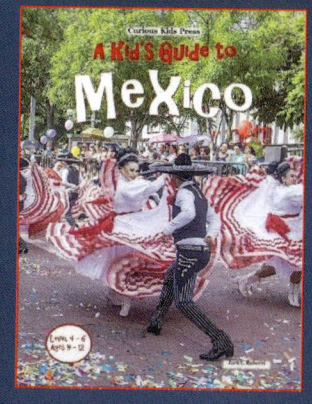

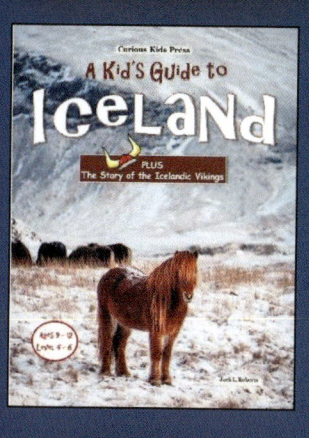

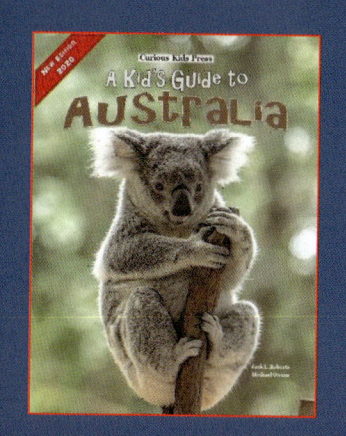

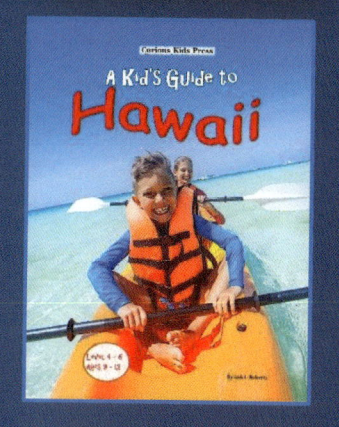

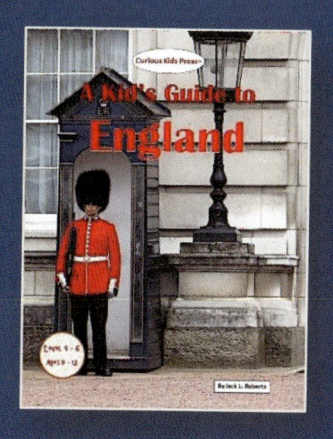

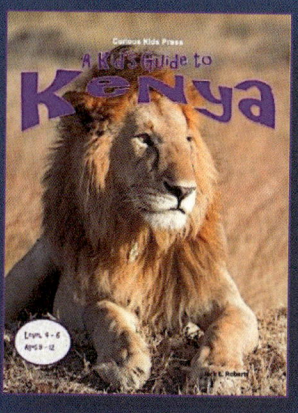

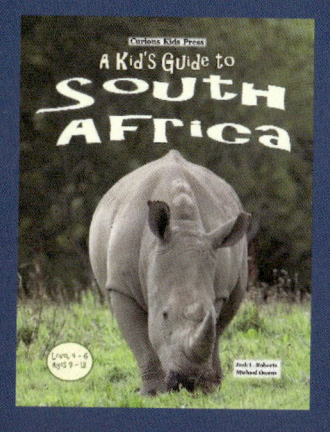

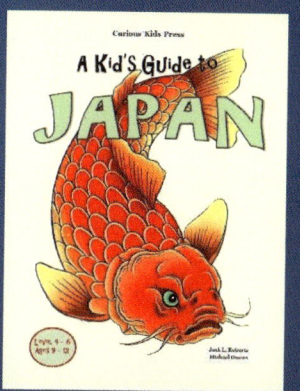

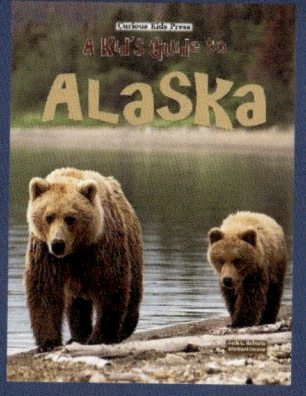

Curious Kids Press
www.curiouskidspress.com

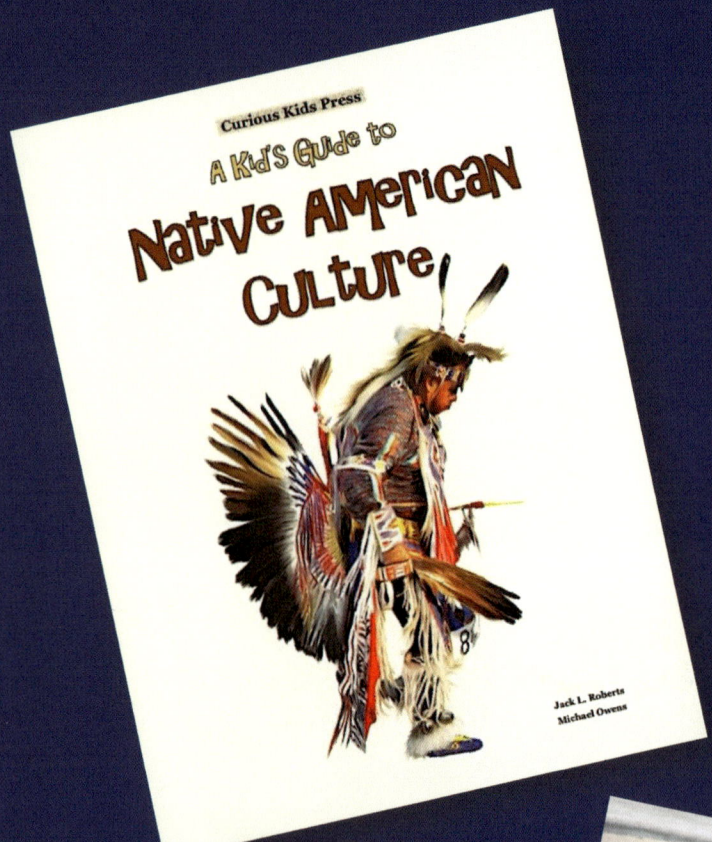

Two important new books for all young readers and their families.

Available on amazon.com

A Kid's Guide to
INdia
For Parents and Teachers

About This Book

A Kid's Guide to . . . is an engaging, easy-to-read book series that provides an exciting adventure into fascinating countries and cultures around the world for young readers. Each book focuses on one country, continent, or U.S. territory or state, and includes colorful photographs, informational charts and graphs, and quirky and bizarre "Did You Know" facts, all designed to bring the country and its people to life. Designed primarily for recreational, high-interest reading, the informational text series is also a great resource for students to use to research geography topics or writing assignments.

About the Reading Level

A Kid's Guide to . . . is an informational text series designed for kids in grades 4 to 6, ages 9 to 12. For some young readers, the series will provide new reading challenges based on the vocabulary and sentence structure. For other readers, the series will review and reinforce reading skills already achieved. While for still other readers, the book will match their current skill level, regardless of age or grade level.

About the Authors

Jack L. Roberts began his career in educational publishing at Children's Television Workshop (now Sesame Workshop), where he was Senior Editor of The Sesame Street/Electric Company Reading Kits. Later, at Scholastic Inc., he was the founding editor of a high-interest/low-reading level magazine for middle school students. He also founded two technology magazines for teachers and administrators.

Roberts is the author of more than two dozen biographies and other nonfiction titles for young readers, published by Scholastic Inc., the Lerner Publishing Group, Teacher Created Materials, Benchmark Education, and others.. More recently, he was the co-founder of WordTeasers, an educational series of card decks designed to help kids of all ages improve their vocabulary through "conversation, not memorization."

Michael Owens is a noted jazz dance teacher, award-winning wildlife photographer, graphic arts designer, and devoted animal lover.

In 2017, Roberts and Owens launched Curious Kids Press (CKP), an educational publishing company focused on publishing high-interest, nonfiction books for young readers, primarily books about countries and cultures around the world. Currently, CKP has published two series of country books: "A Kid's Guide to..." (for ages 9-12 and "Let's Visit . . ." (for ages 6-8) — both designed to help young readers explore the wonderful world of diversity in everything from food and holidays to geography and traditions.

To Our Valued Customers

Curious Kids Press is passionate about creating fun-to-read books about countries and cultures around the world for young readers, and we work hard every day to create quality products.

All of our books are Print on Demand books. As a result, on rare occasions, you may find minor printing errors. If you feel you have not received a quality printed product, please send us a description and photo of the printing error along with your name and address and we will have a new copy sent to you free of charge. Contact us at: info@curiouskidspress.com

Printed in Great Britain
by Amazon